Color-n-Doodle Your World:
A Can Find Happy Adult Coloring Book

© 2019 by Ranch House Press. All rights reserved.

Printed in the United States of America.

www.annettebridges.com

ISBN–13: 978-1-946371-45-4

Color-N-Doodle
YOUR WORLD

I N T R O D U C T I O N

I've labeled the Color-n-Doodle Your World as a "can find happy" adult coloring book. That's because this year my word of intention is *happy*. I've been in a long, rough season of caregiving of loved ones who eventually succumbed to aging and illnesses. In the midst, I found stress relief in the relaxing art of coloring. It was helpful to nurture my soul with moments that self-soothed my weariness. Playing with colors made me happy. I learned it was possible to feel happy while still feeling so very sad.

During times when life feels gloomy or overwhelming, you need and deserve a break and time-out from adult struggles and problems.

There are simple pleasures to be enjoyed at every season in our life. And coloring and doodling are some of those pleasures. And more than pleasure, coloring and doodling really can provide you with a legitimate form of therapy and meditation. I certainly hope you find it as healing and comforting as I have!

Love,
Annette Bridges

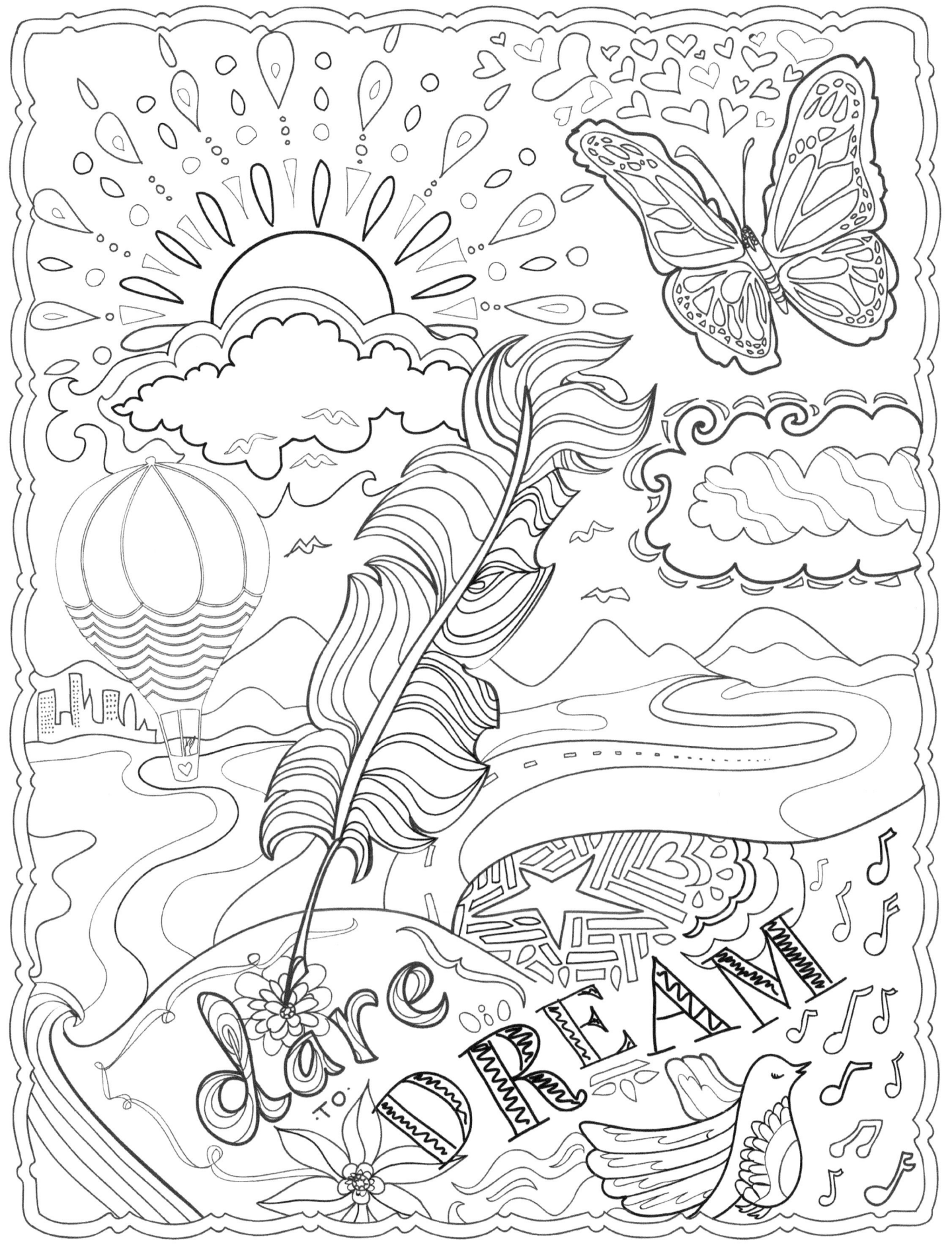

color-n-doodle your world

color-n-doodle your world

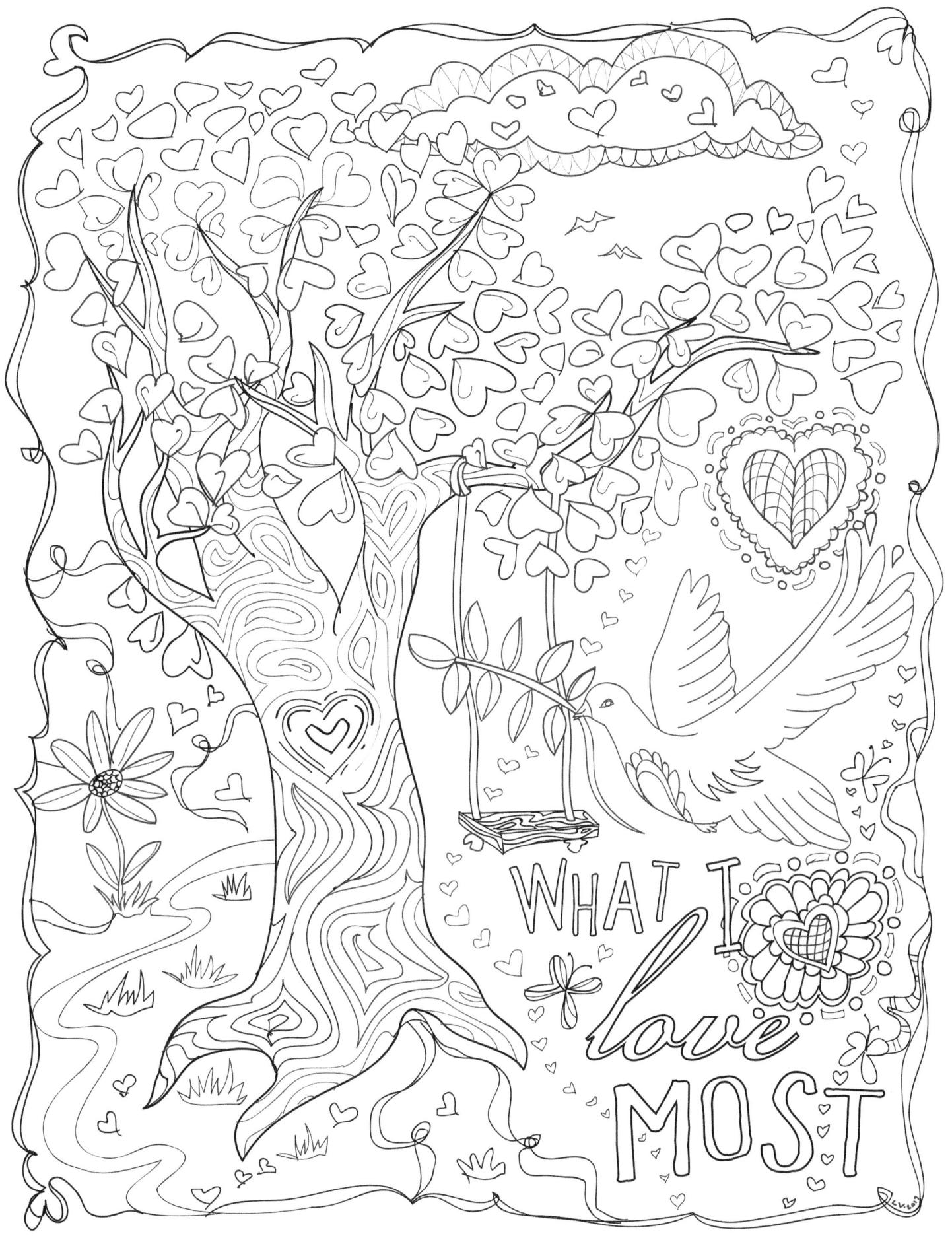

color-n-doodle your world

color-n-doodle your world

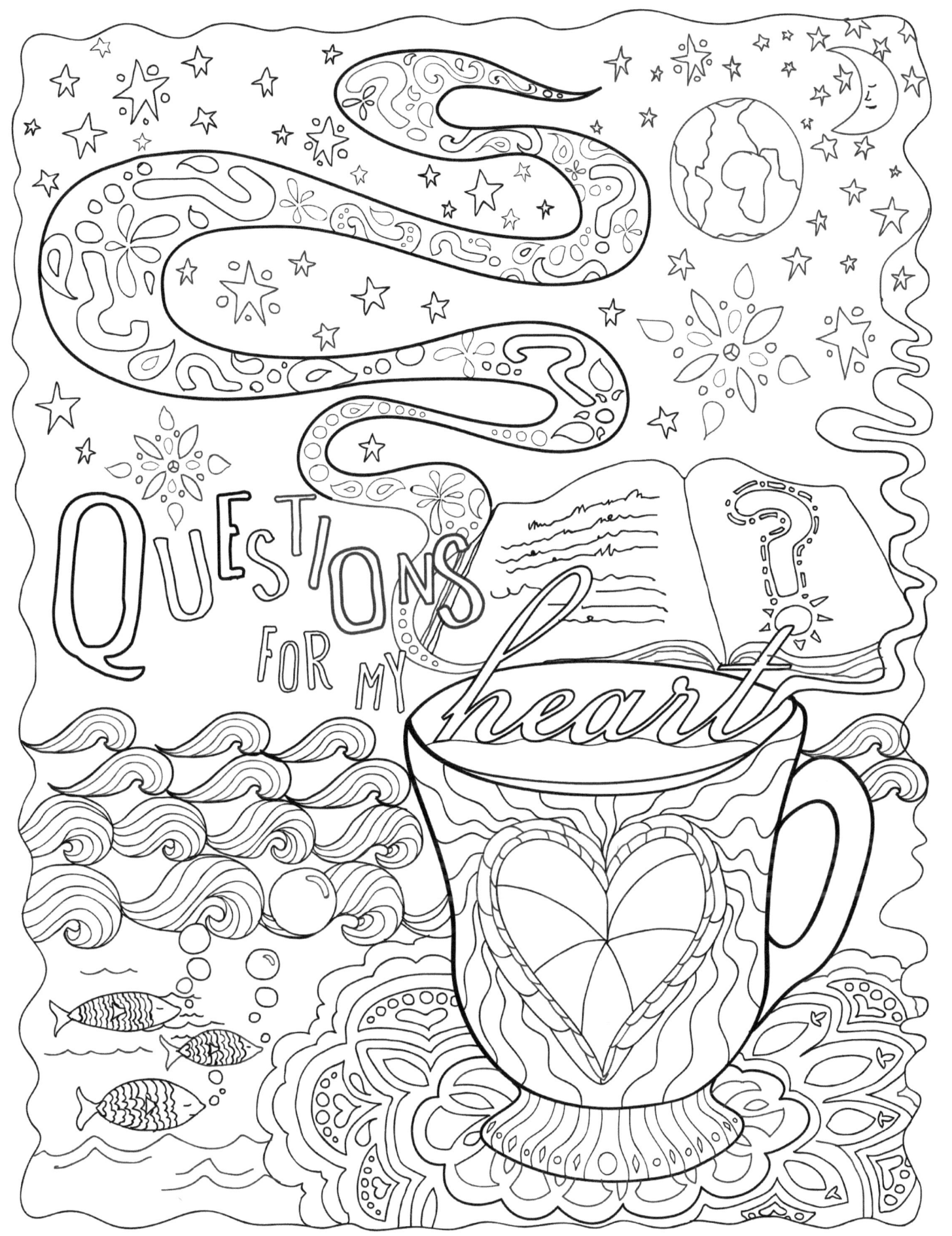

color-n-doodle your world

color-n-doodle your world

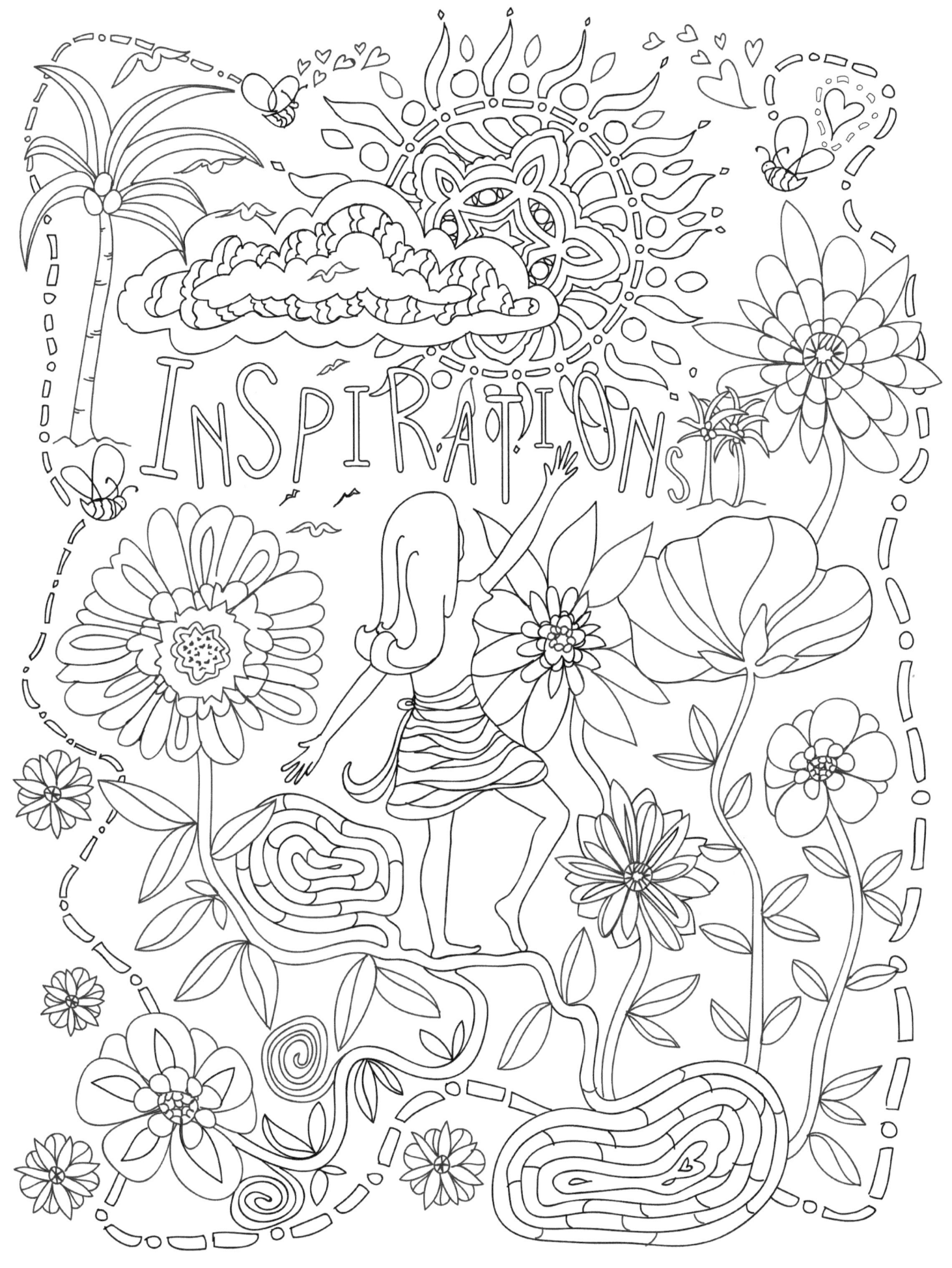

color-n-doodle your world

color-n-doodle your world

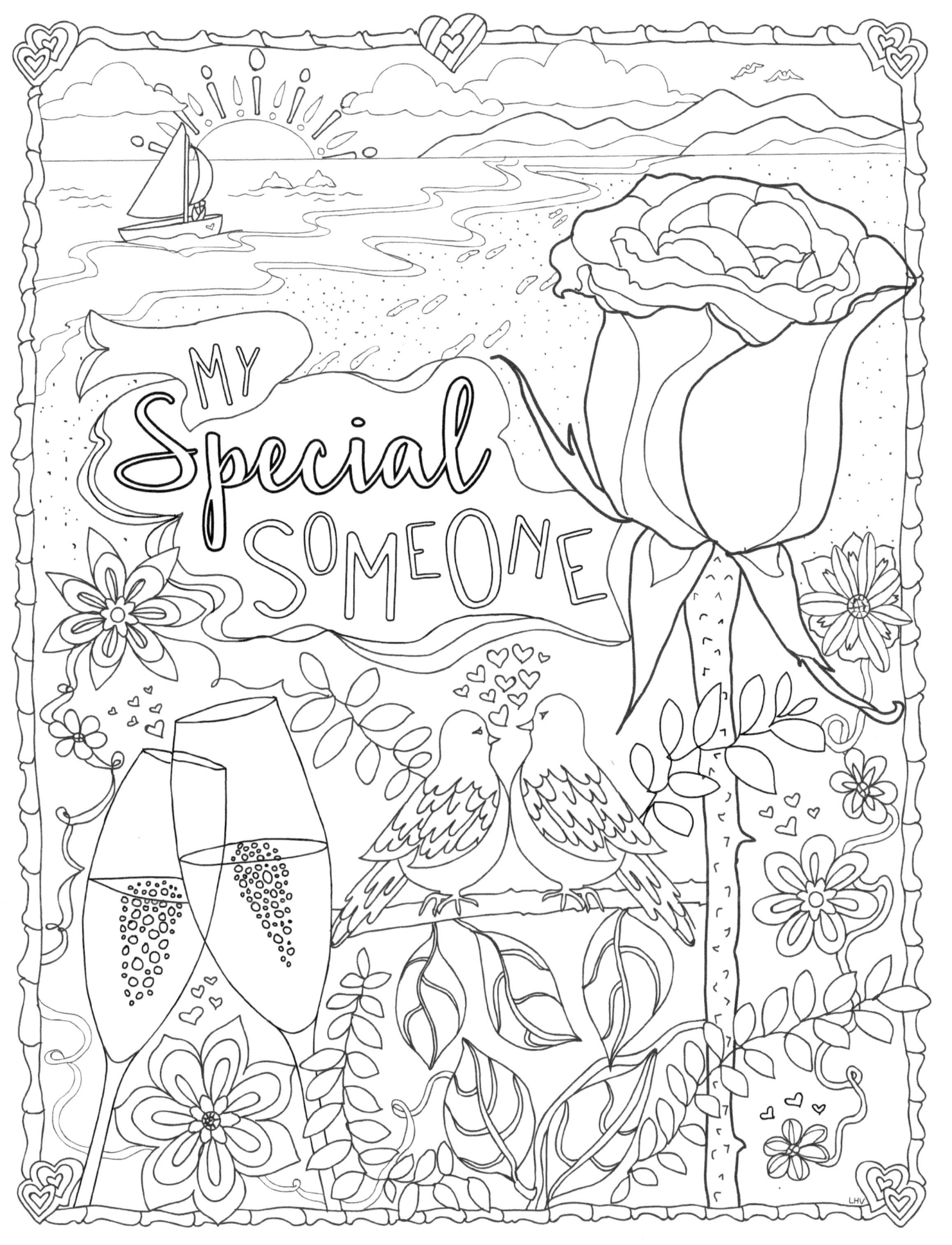

color-n-doodle your world

color-n-doodle your world

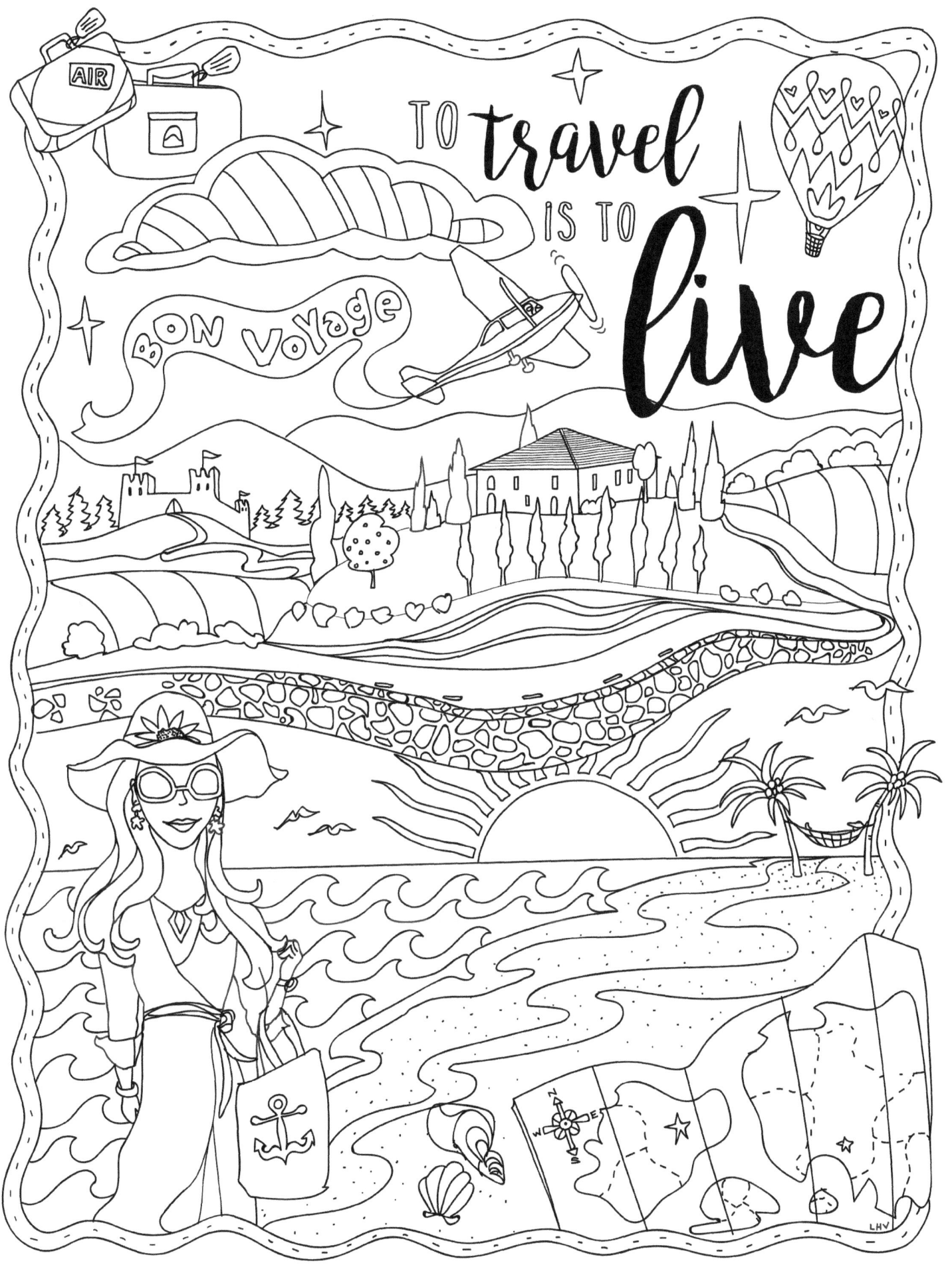

color-n-doodle your world

color-n-doodle your world

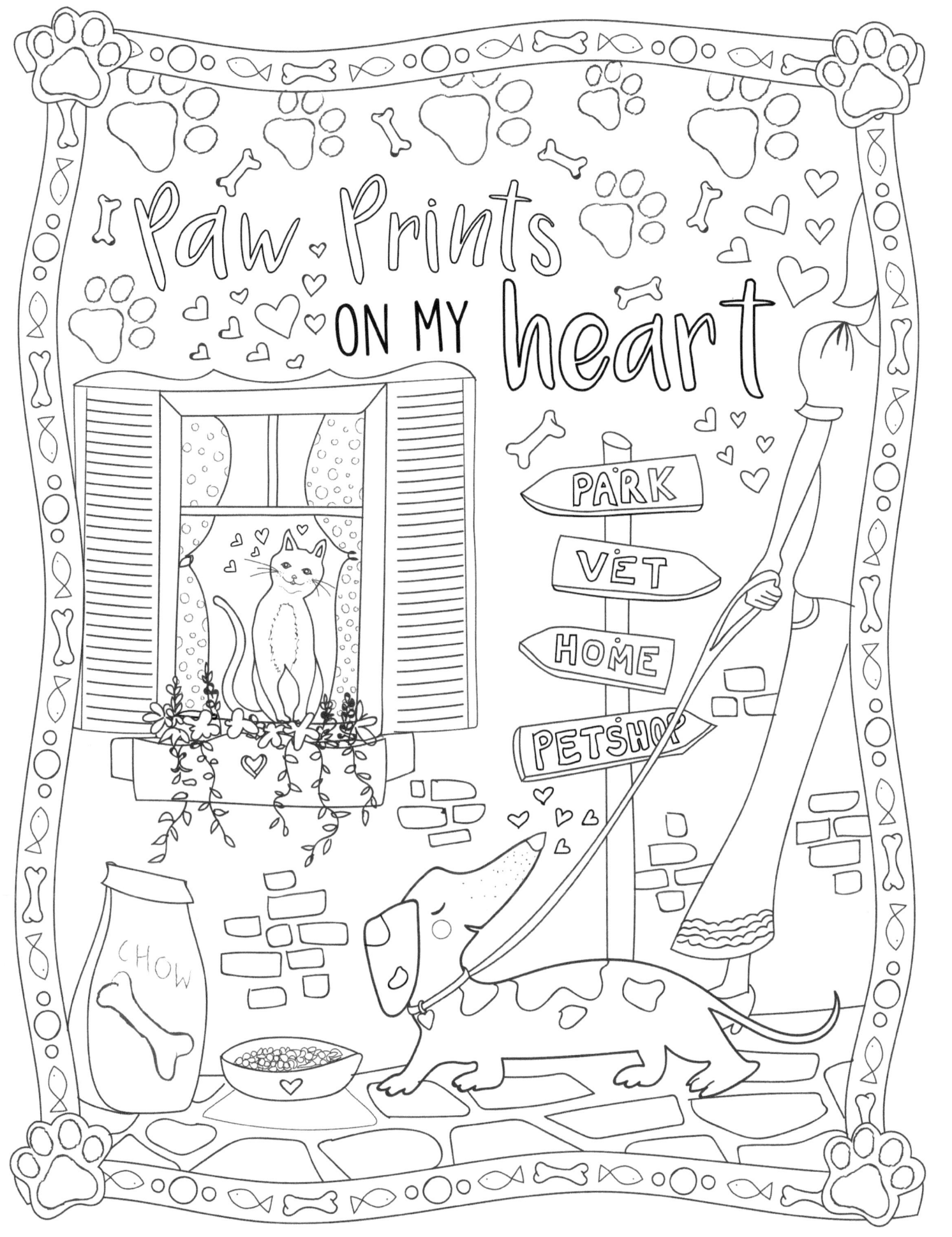

color-n-doodle your world

color-n-doodle your world

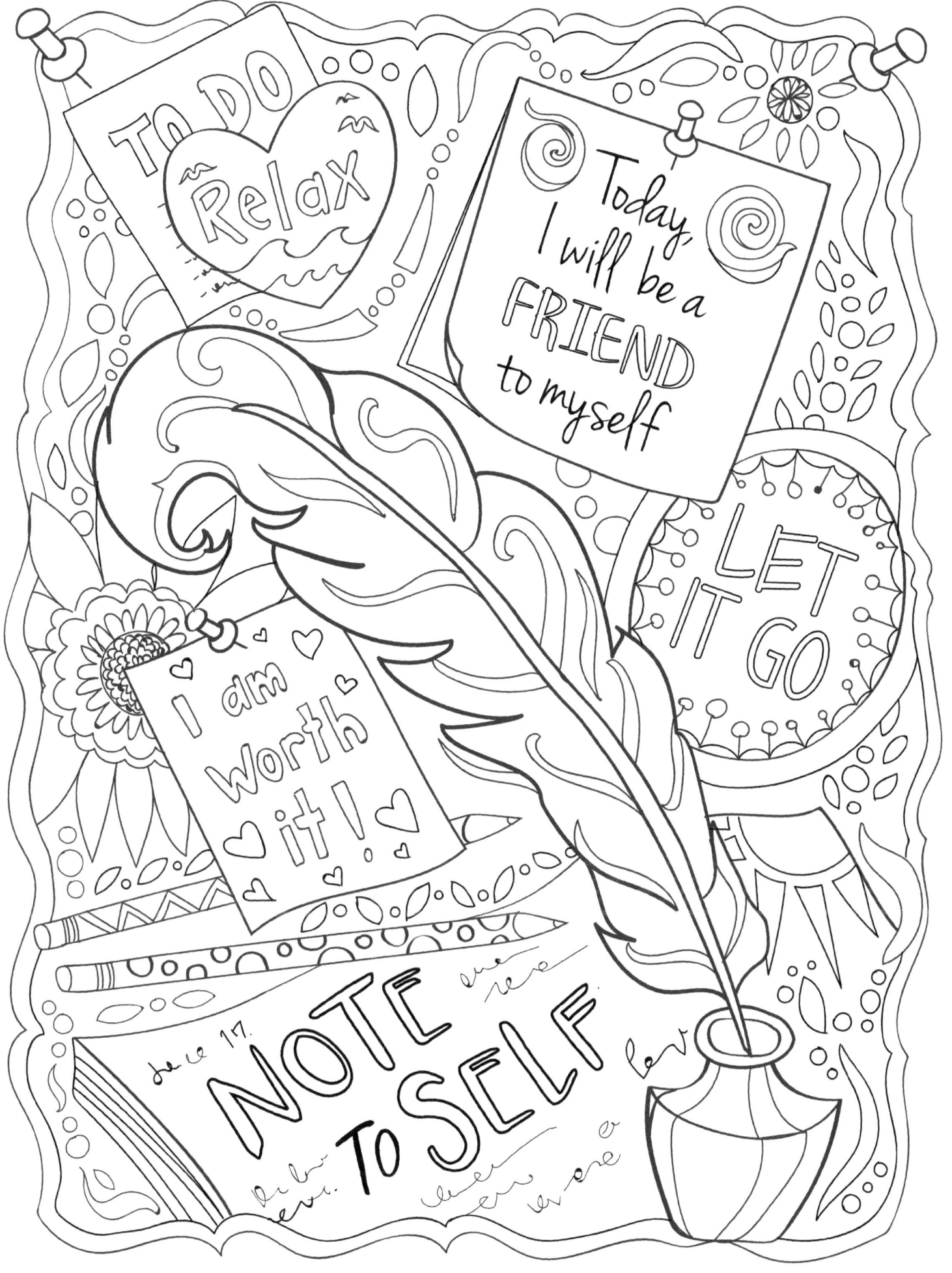

color-n-doodle your world

color-n-doodle your world

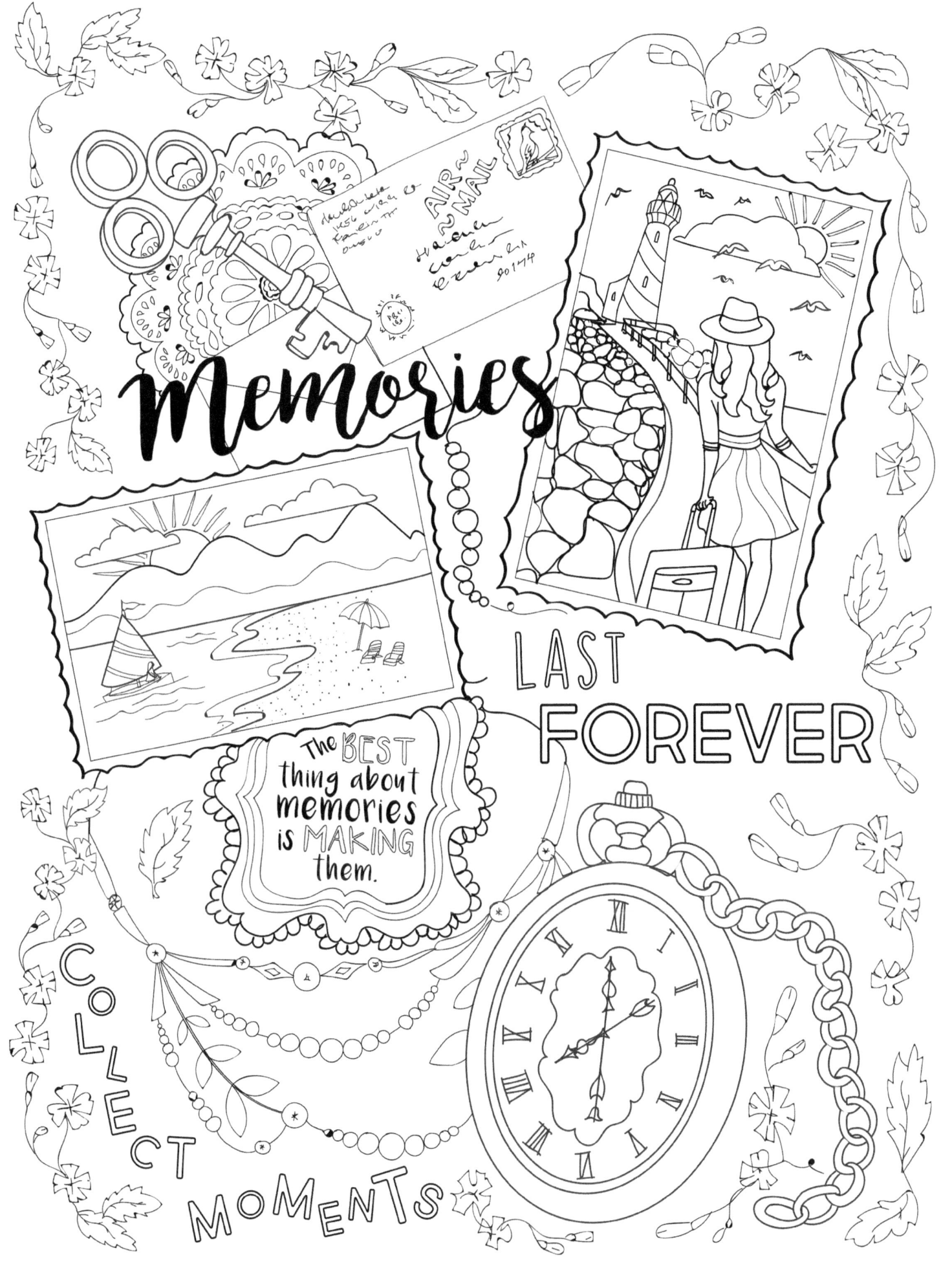

color-n-doodle your world

color-n-doodle your world

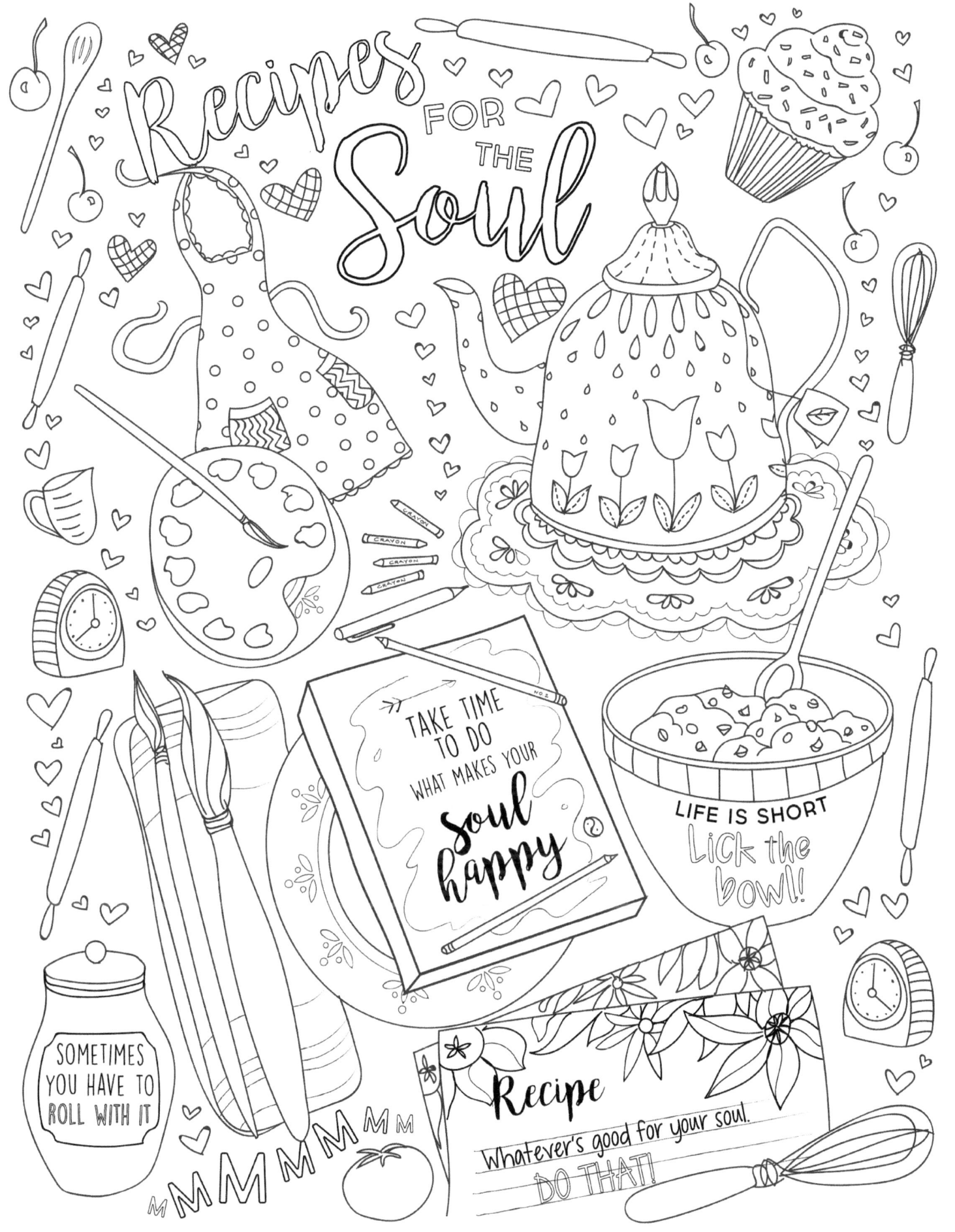

color-n-doodle your world

color-n-doodle your world

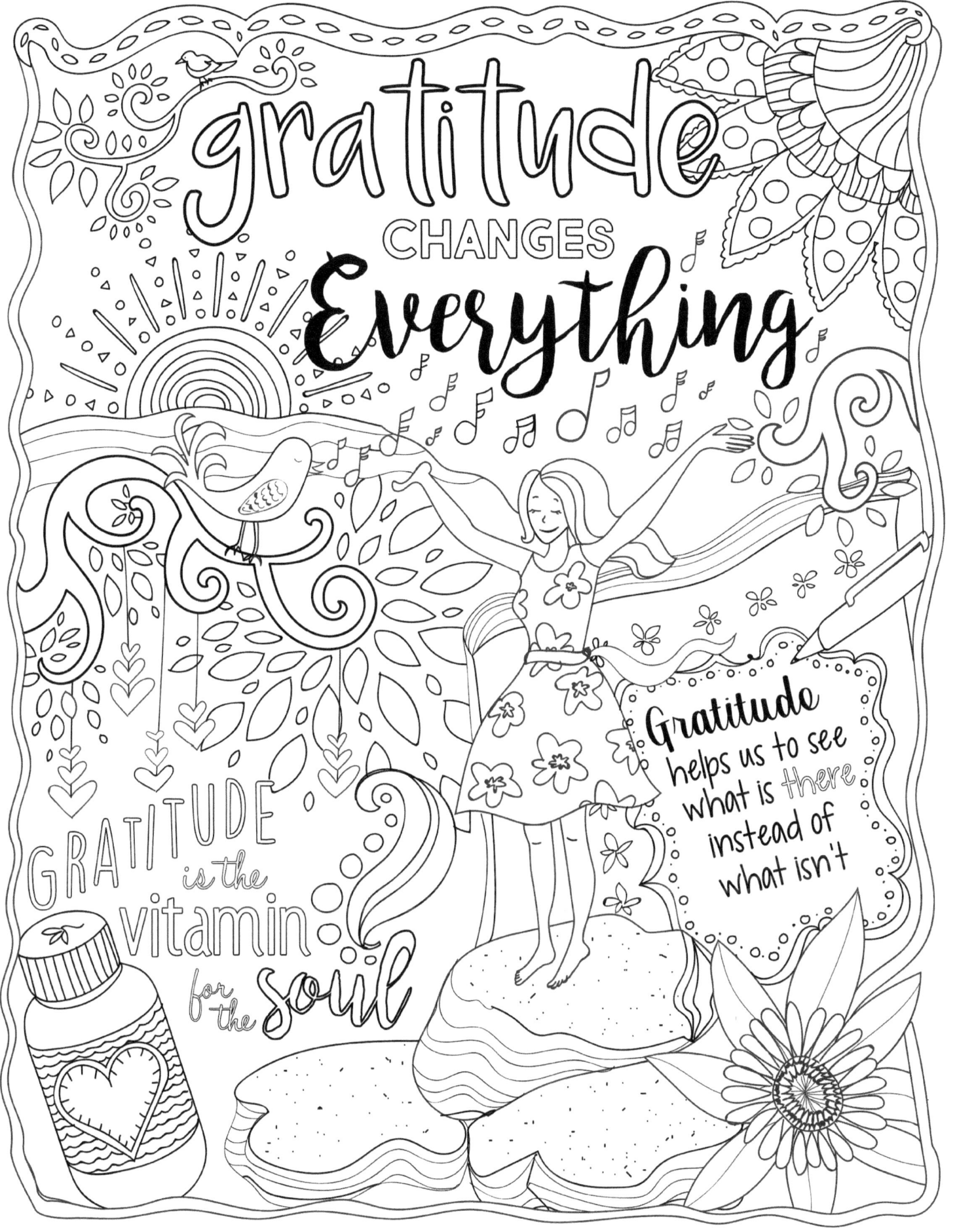

color-n-doodle your world

color-n-doodle your world

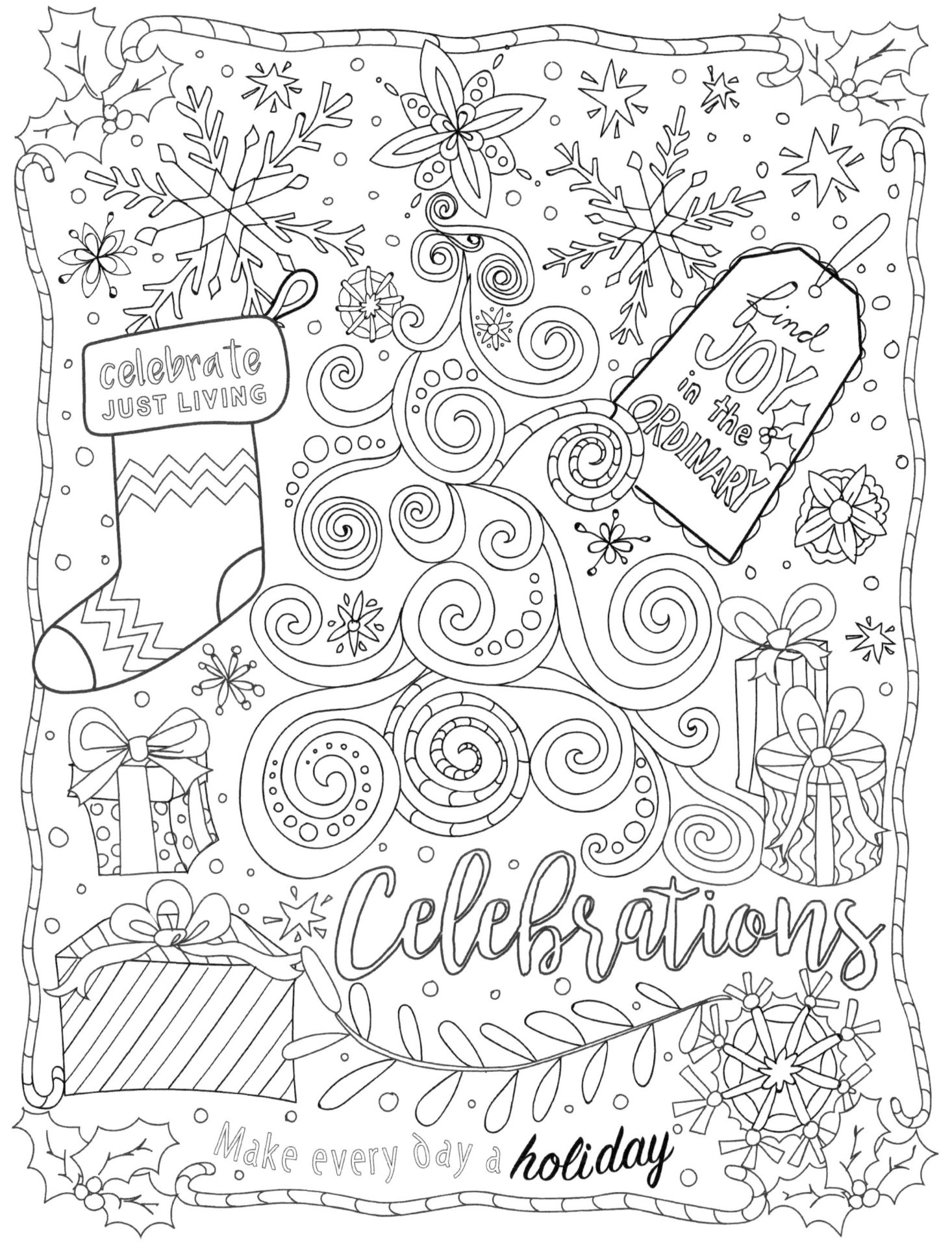

color-n-doodle your world

color-n-doodle your world

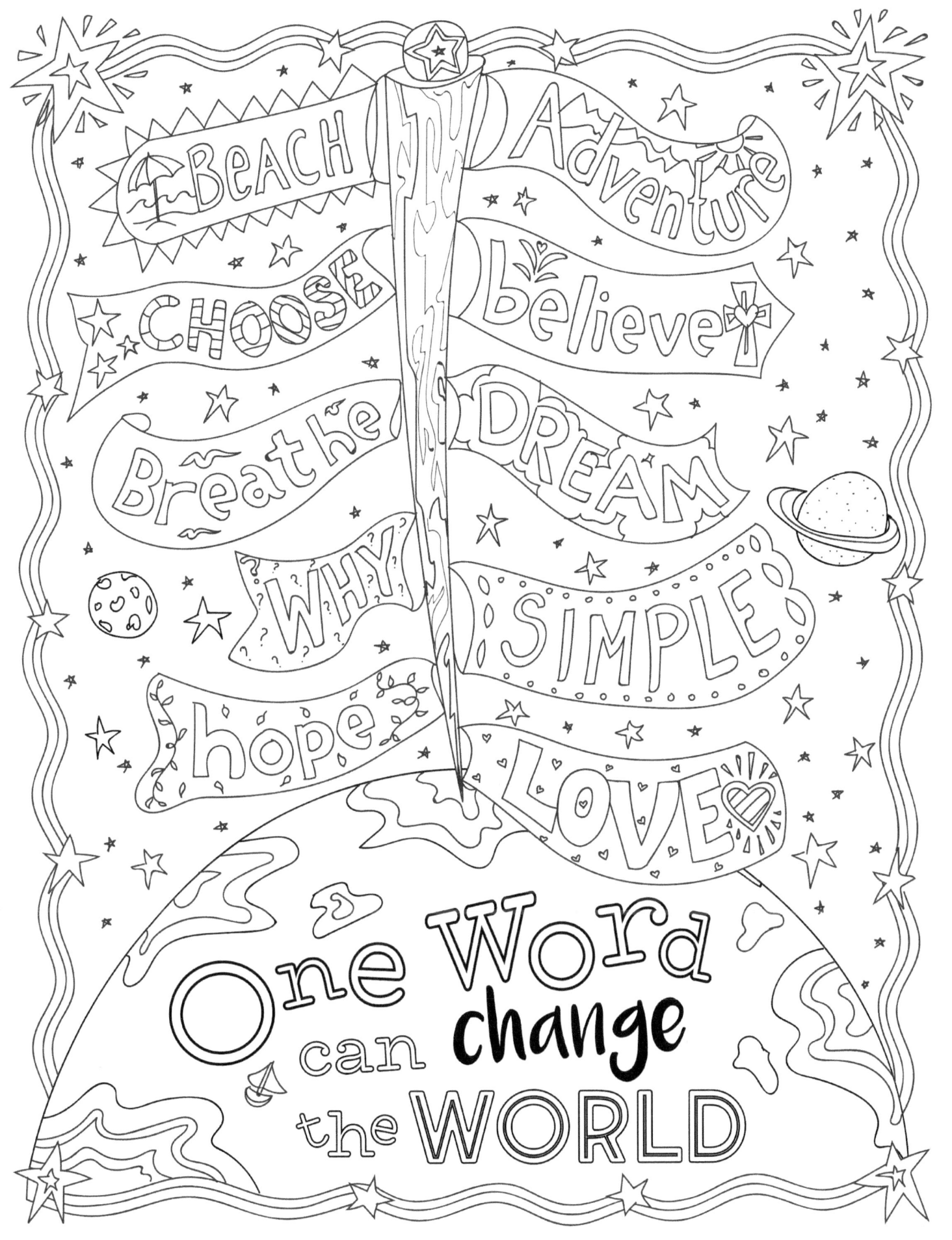

color-n-doodle your world

color-n-doodle your world

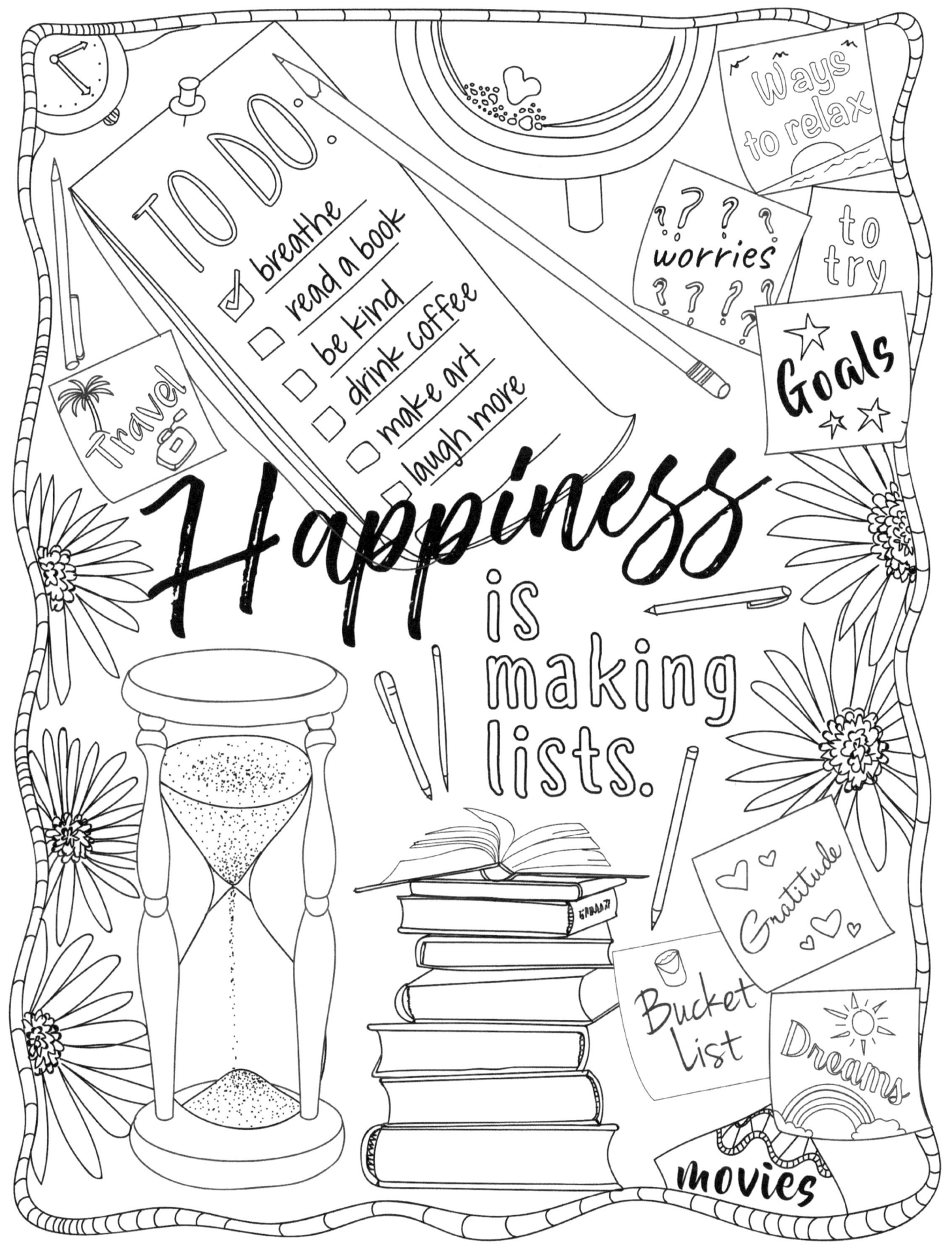

color-n-doodle your world

color-n-doodle your world

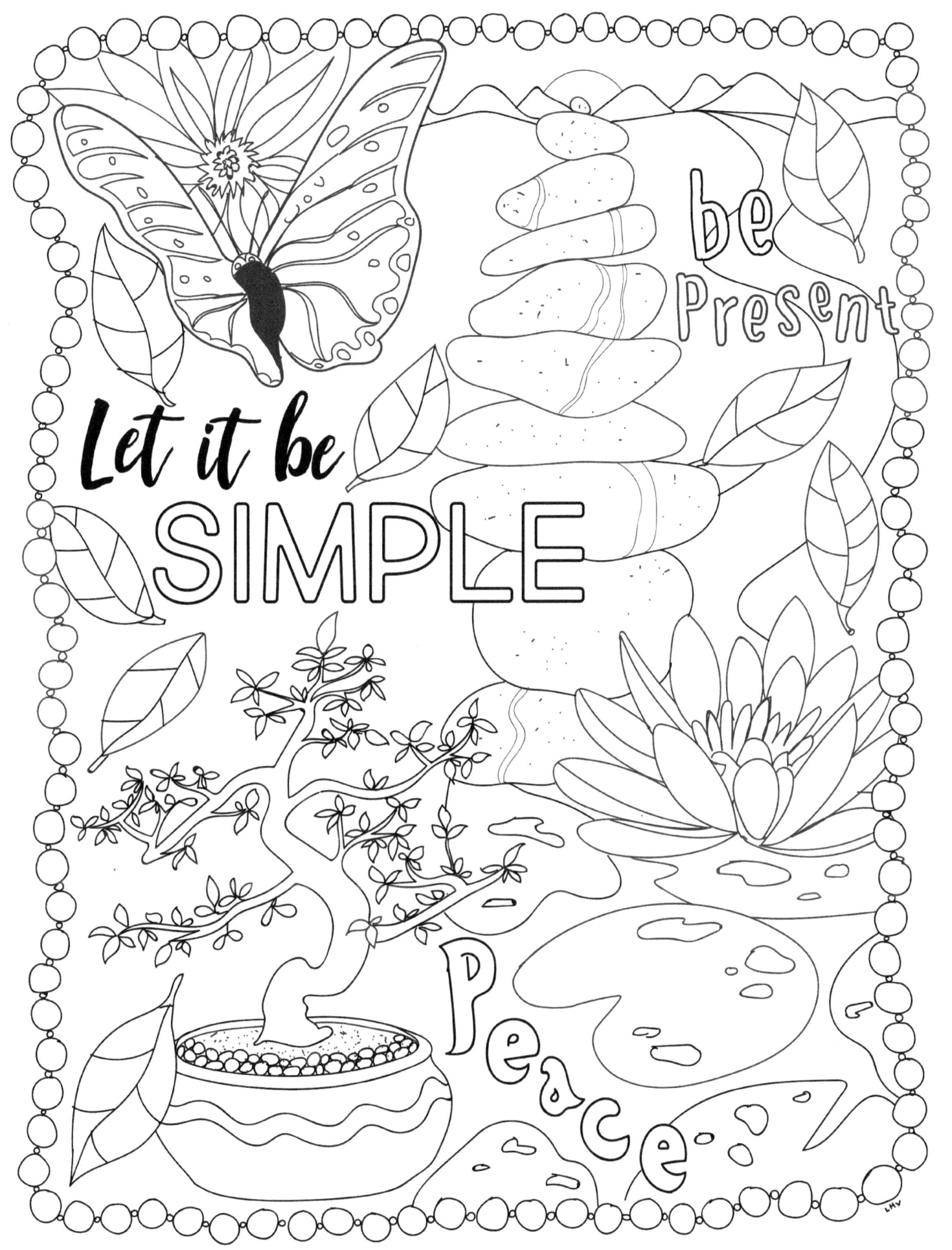

color-n-doodle your world

color-n-doodle your world

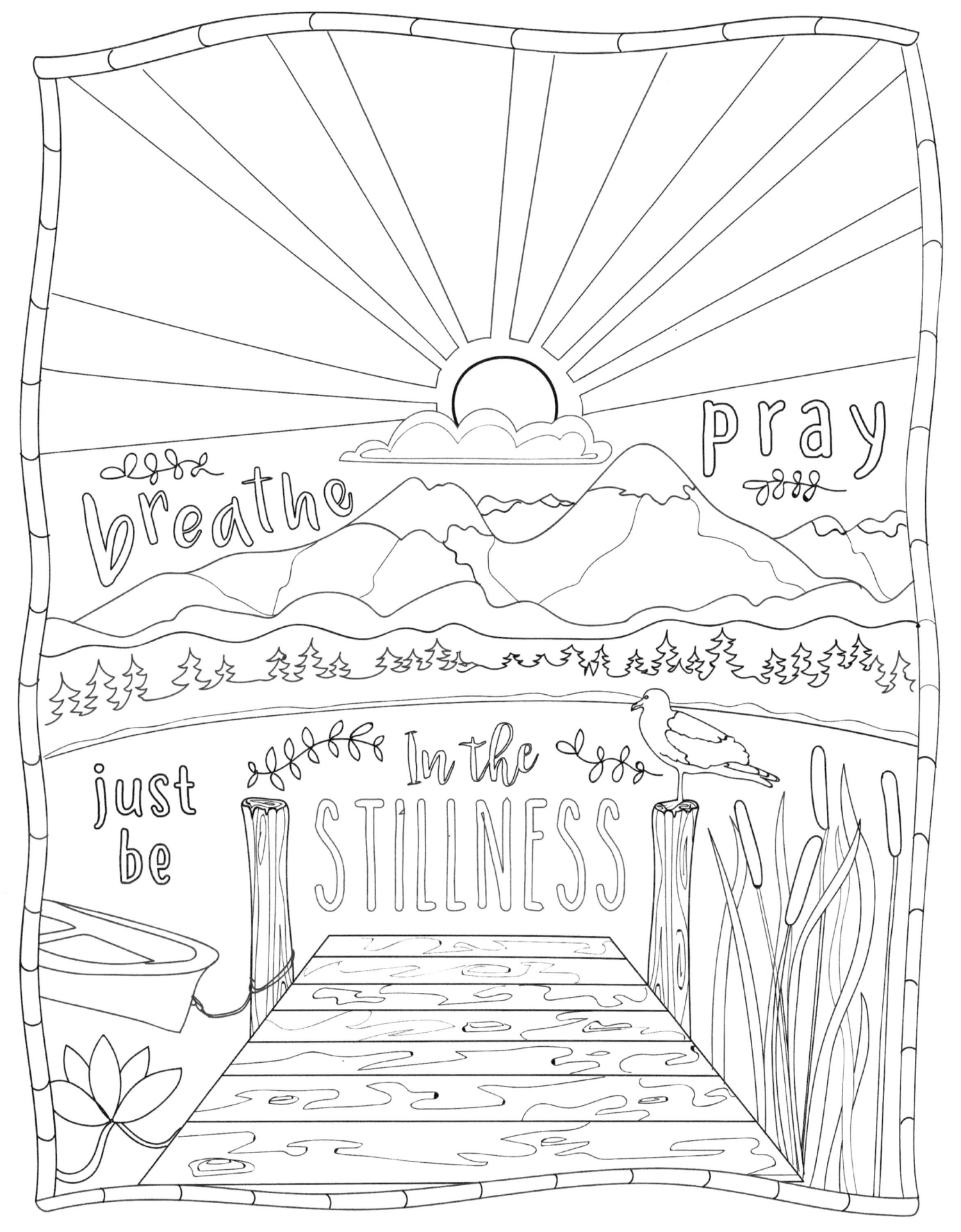

color-n-doodle your world

color-n-doodle your world

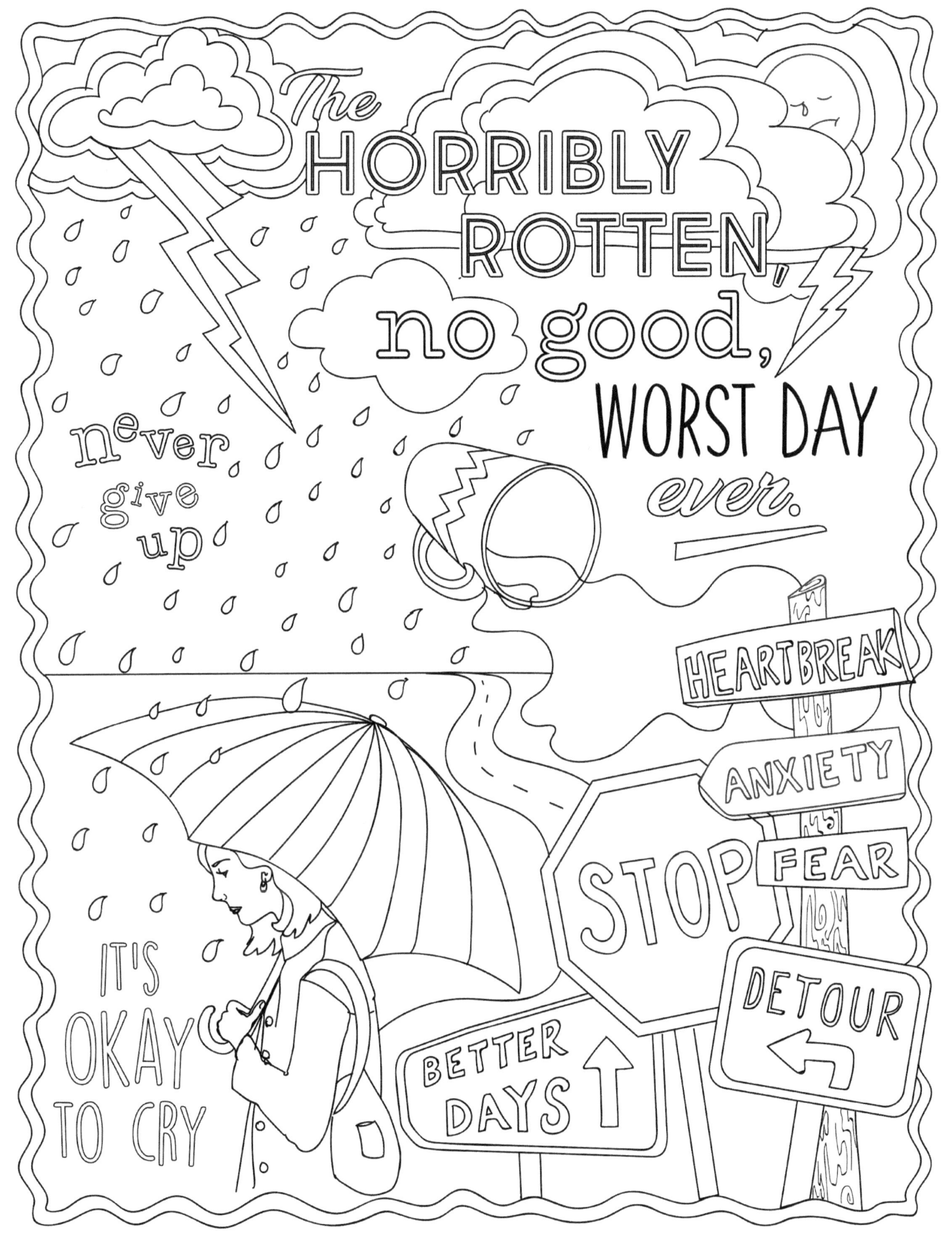

color-n-doodle your world

color-n-doodle your world

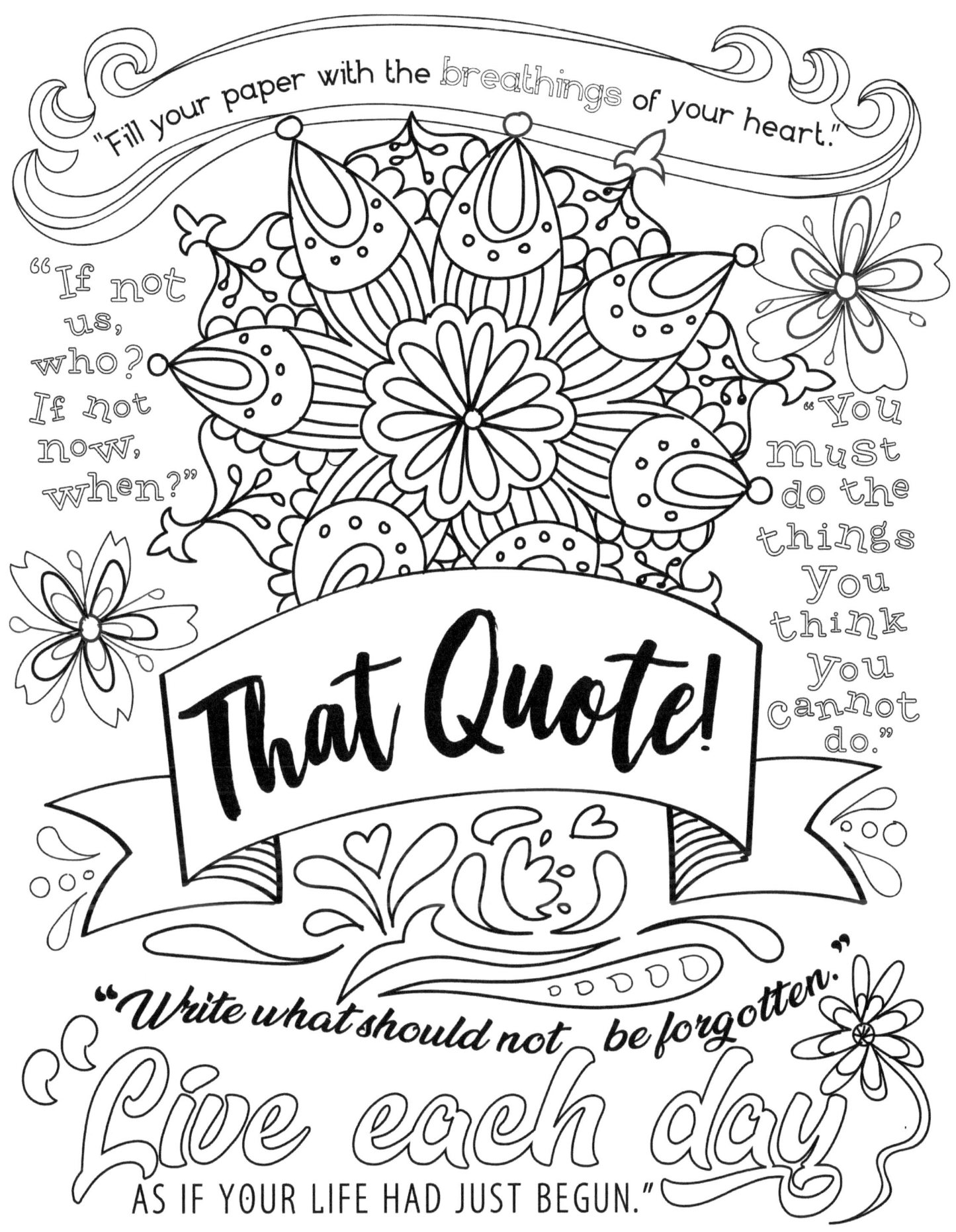

color-n-doodle your world

color-n-doodle your world

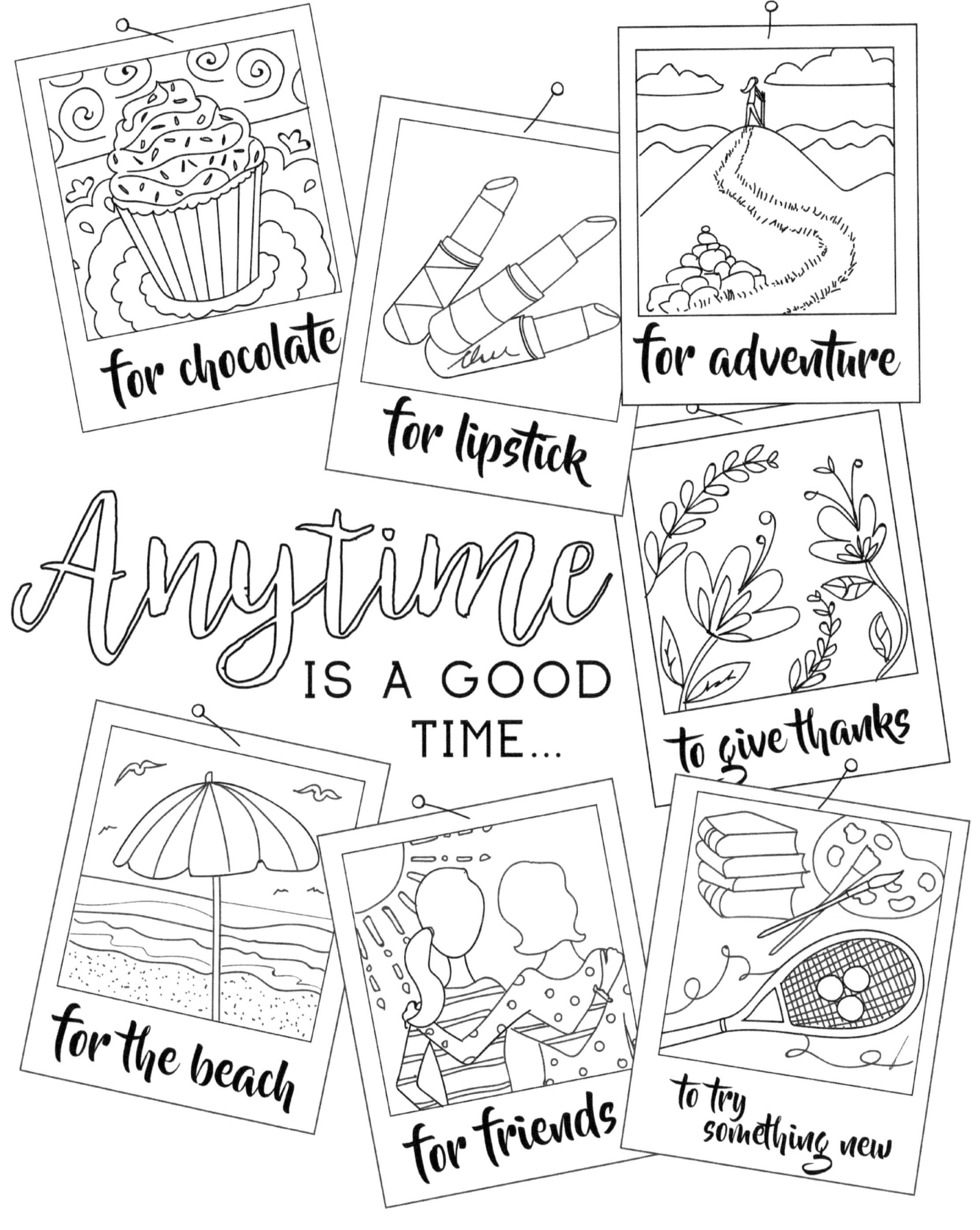

color-n-doodle your world

color-n-doodle your world

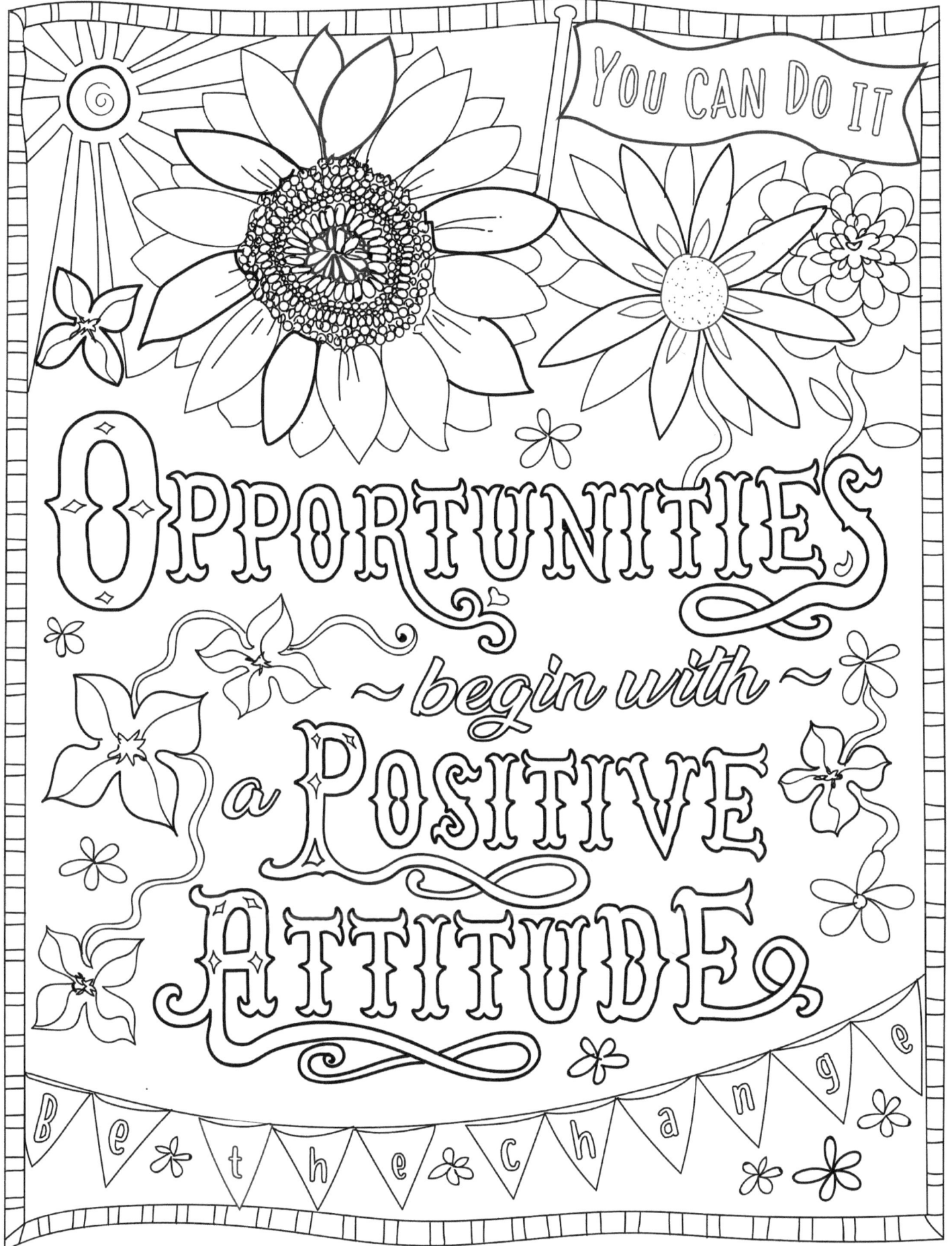

color-n-doodle your world

color-n-doodle your world

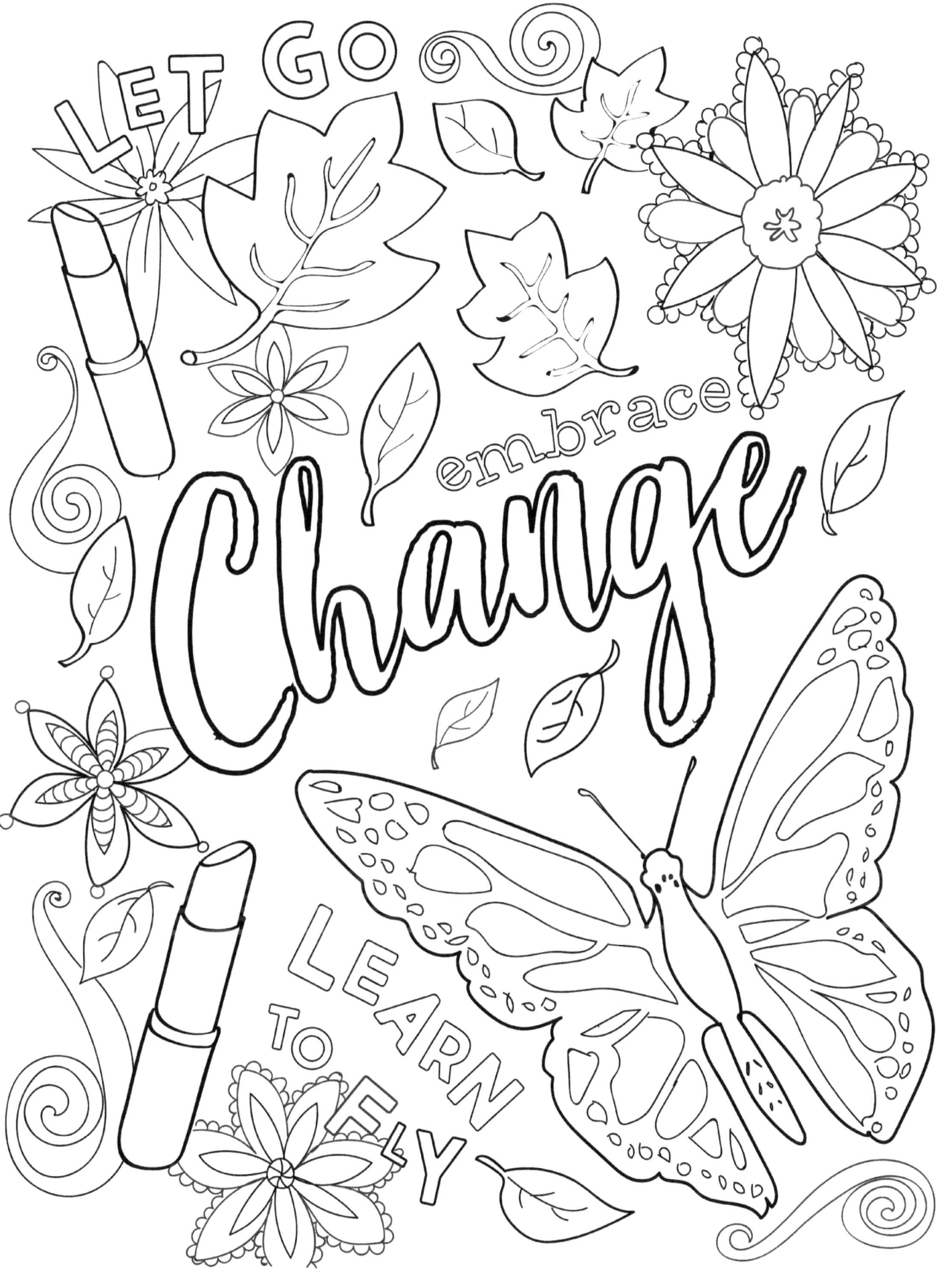

color-n-doodle your world

color-n-doodle your world

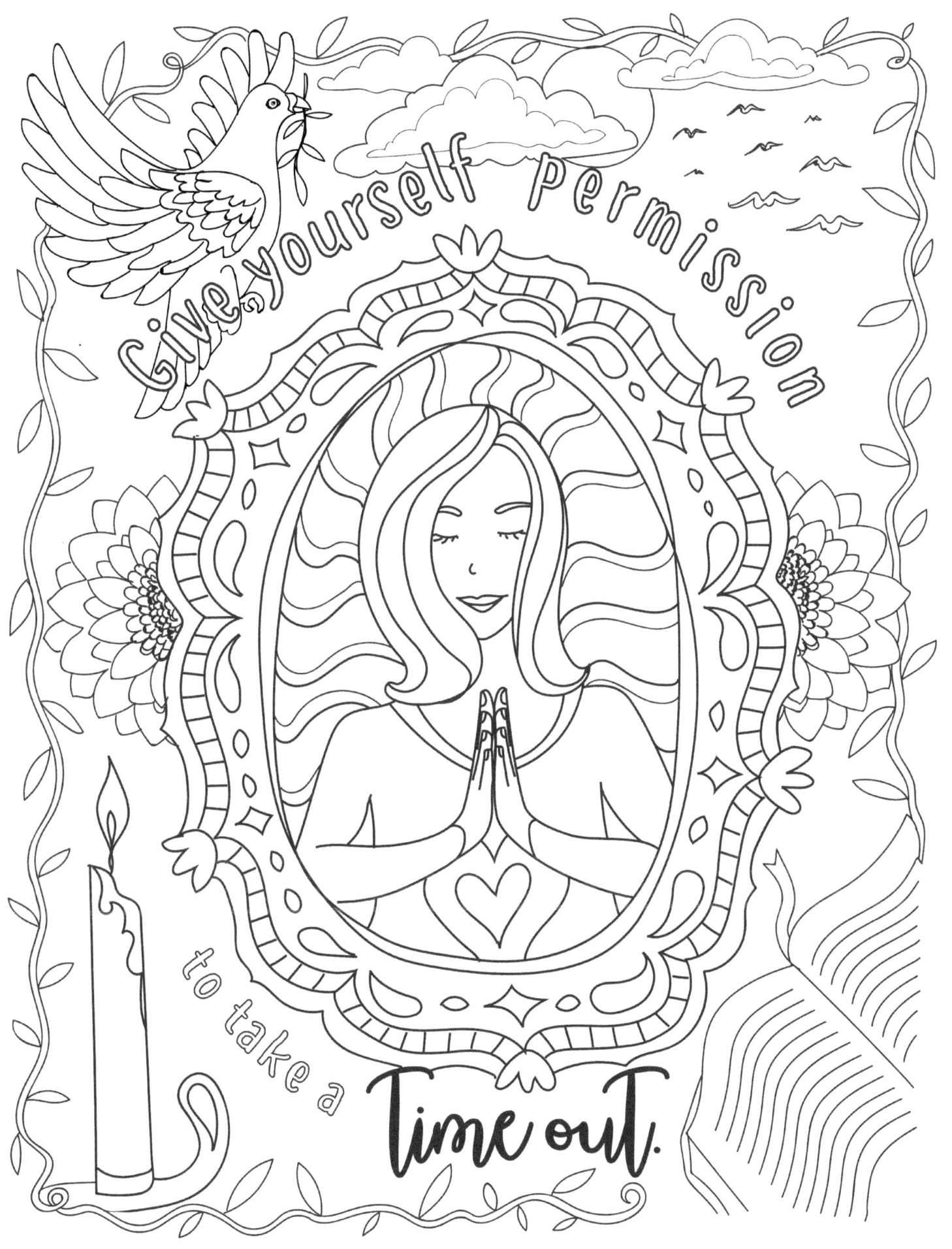

color-n-doodle your world

color-n-doodle your world

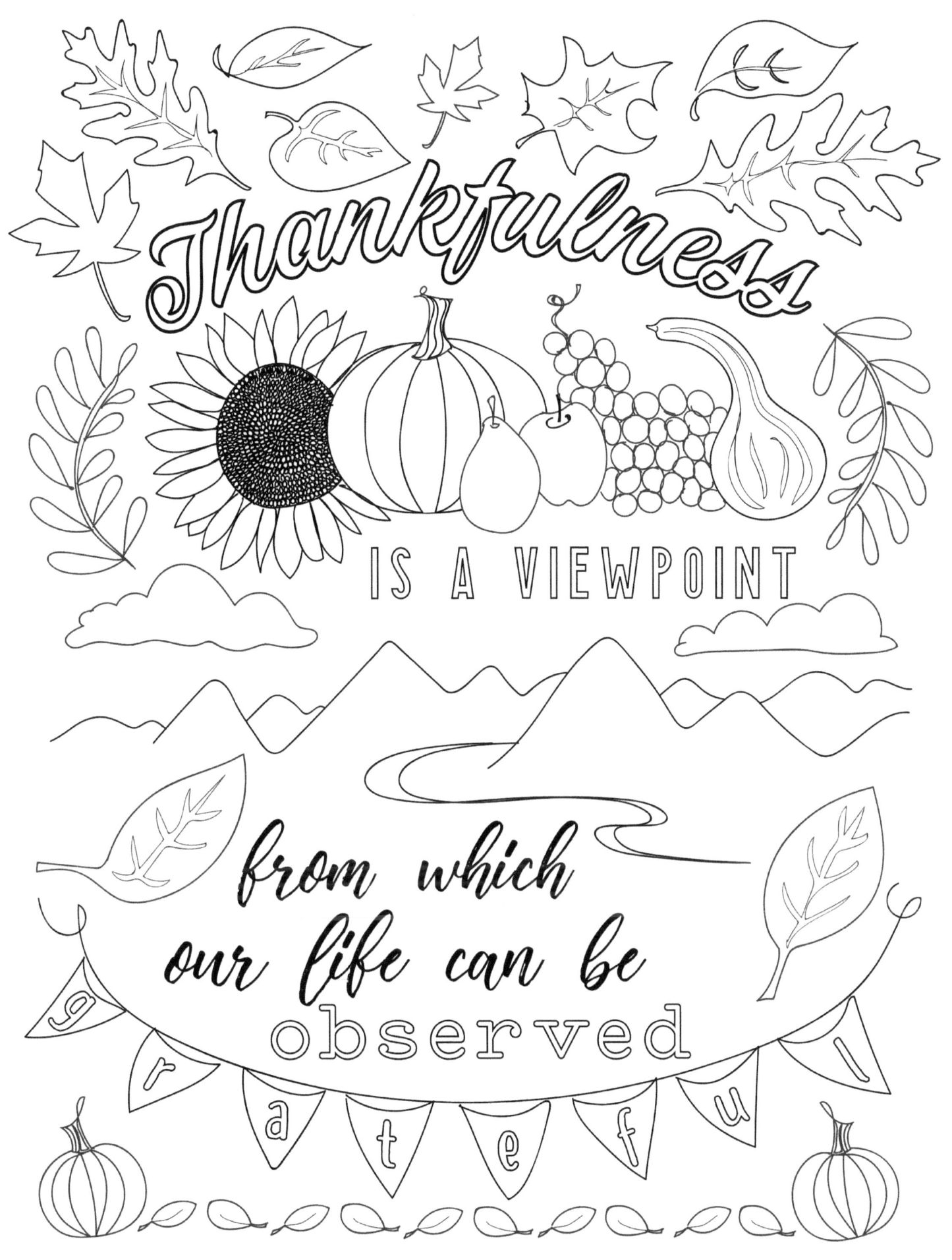

color-n-doodle your world

color-n-doodle your world

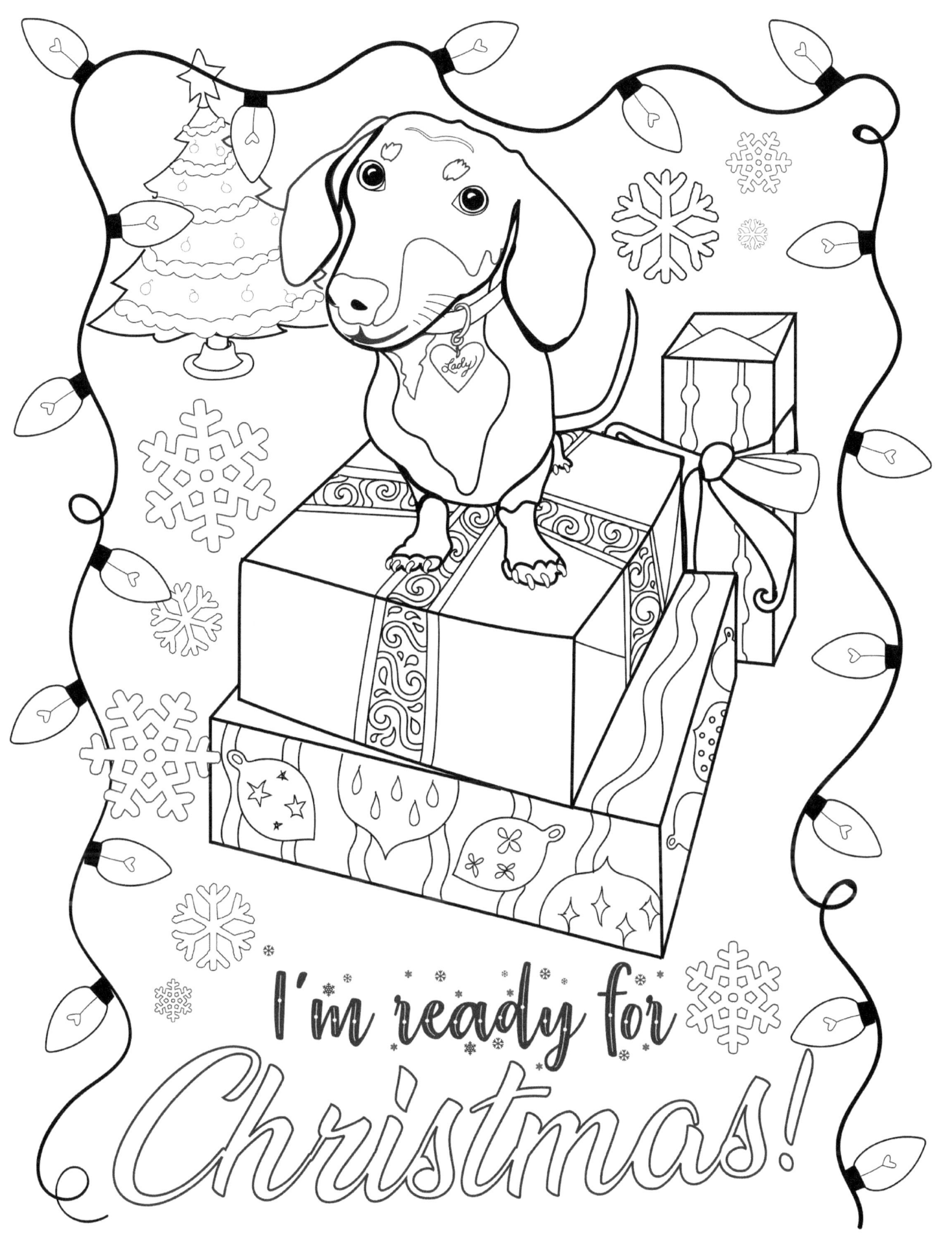

color-n-doodle your world

color-n-doodle your world

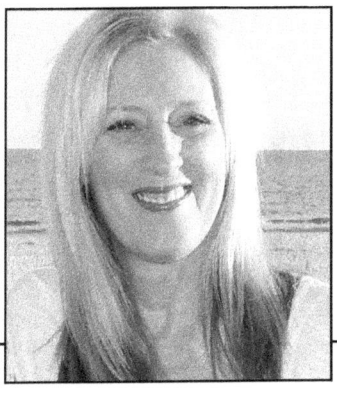

Annette Bridges
ABOUT THE AUTHOR/CREATOR

Annette Bridges is an author and founder of Ranch House Press, a publisher of books, journals and more that empower, encourage, and entertain. She has published nonfiction books, coloring books, journals and even a cookbook for children. She's also a women's retreat host, cattle rancher's wife, and college professor's mom. Annette's mission is to help every woman realize that HER STORY is extraordinary, valuable, and noteworthy. Before writing books, this former public and homeschool educator spent a decade writing instructive and light-hearted columns for Texas newspapers, magazines, and websites. Today, Annette writes a monthly lifestyle column titled "When a city girl goes country" for *North Texas Farm and Ranch Magazine.*

Annette has spoken at women's conferences and retreats, chamber events and senior living facilities. She loves to do book readings, meet the author events, and book club groups. These days, Annette's favorite speaking topics include talking about the art of aging as learned from her very sassy, southern mamma and lessons learned from her dog and how writing about them helped her with grieving the death of her beloved seventeen-year-old dachshund.

Annette lives on a North Texas cattle ranch with her husband, John. She can drive a tractor but only if she's wearing a fresh coat of lipstick and it's not her pedicure day!

You can learn more about Annette at her website: www.annettebridges.com and by following her Texas author page on Facebook. She is available for in-person and virtual events and interviews.

A L S O   B Y   A N N E T T E

My Furry Friend
A Keepsake Journal.

A Dachshund Tale
Lessons Learned from My Dog.

Color Your World Journal Series
18 each Themed Niche Journals and Jot Journals.

Oh, how the years fly by!
A whimsical coloring journey. An adult coloring book.

Oh, how the years fly by!
A whimsical inspirational journey. A quote book.

The Gospel According to Mamma
One mother's philosophy on love, money, God, aging, decisions, change, and much more.

Be Queen of Your Life
A savvy mom helps daughters command and rule their lives.

Have Lipstick, Will Travel
How to reimagine your life, purpose & hair color.

Lady and Bella
Totally Different, Totally Friends. A coloring storybook for children

Lady and Bella
Totally friends journal. Especially for children.

Lady and Bella's Alphabet Kitchen
A to Z Recipes for Kid Cooks.

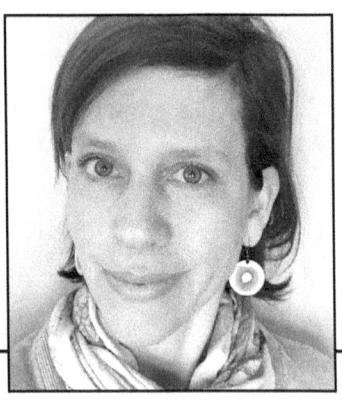

Lesley Vernon
ABOUT THE ILLUSTRATOR

Lesley Vernon is an illustrator, graphic designer, and fine artist. She has illustrated several children's coloring books and a number of other book covers, marketing materials, and print designs. In addition, Lesley loves sketching, drawing in pen & ink, and dabbles in watercolor too.

Lesley, along with her husband and two sons, lives in southeastern Massachusetts. She spends her free time hiking and camping in the woods and mountains of New England, exploring the rocky coast of Maine and raising a flock of backyard chickens.

She and her family enjoy making art together, and she hopes people everywhere will love coloring in this book!

To find out more about Lesley's work, please visit her website at:
www.lvdesignhouse.com

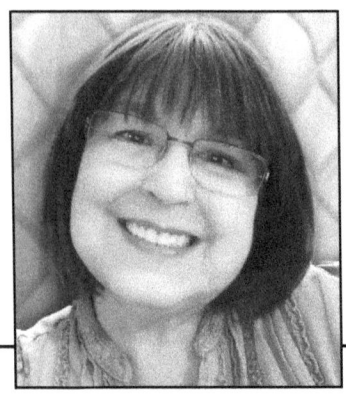

Janie Owen-Bugh
ABOUT THE DESIGNER

A recent graduate of the Art Institute of Dallas, Janie Owen-Bugh's career actually started several decades ago. She's made a name for herself with her attention to detail, out-of-the box ideas, technical savvy, and problem solving ability.

Throughout her career, she has designed numerous print and digital materials for a variety of industries. Having developed a love for the publishing industry in recent years she has designed dozens of books and over 50 book covers.

She lives in a suburb of Dallas, TX and enjoys spending time with her two granddaughters, painting, singing, and traveling.

To see more of Janie's work, please visit her website at:
janieowenbugh.com